# LIBRARY LEADERSHIP YOUR WAY

*ALA Editions purchases fund advocacy, awareness, and accreditation programs for library professionals worldwide.*

# LIBRARY LEADERSHIP *your way*

JASON MARTIN

ALA Editions
CHICAGO | 2019

**JASON MARTIN** is associate dean of the James E. Walker Library at Middle Tennessee State University, where he oversees library assessment and professional development. He holds an EdD in educational leadership from the University of Central Florida and an MLS from the University of South Florida. He researches, publishes, and presents on leadership, organizational culture, mindfulness, emotional intelligence, productivity, and goal setting and achievement.

---



ISBN: 978-0-8389-1905-7 (paper)

Library of Congress Cataloging-in-Publication Data on file.

Book design by Alejandra Diaz in the Expo Serif Pro and Interstate typefaces.

∞ This paper meets the requirements of ANSI/NISO Z39.48-1992 (Permanence of Paper).

Printed in the United States of America
23 22 21 20 19 5 4 3 2 1

# contents

*Getting Started* ***vii***

1 **Leadership Self-Analysis** ........ 1

Definition of Leadership **1**

Leadership Traits, Skills, and Abilities **2**

Theory of Leadership **3**

Unique Selling Proposition **7**

Leadership Ambition **8**

2 **Leadership, Followership, and Organizational Culture** ........ 9

Leadership **9**

Followership **13**

Organizational Culture **14**

The Leadership/Followership Process **17**

Your Leadership Experience **18**

3 **Leading Yourself** ........ 21

Leading Yourself Effectively **22**

Self-Care **30**

4 **Leading Others** 35

Leading Others Effectively **35**

Leadership Traits, Skills, and Abilities **41**

Theory X, Y, and Z **45**

Contingency Theory and Situational Leadership **47**

Leader-Member Exchange **50**

Transformational Leadership **52**

Emotional Intelligence **56**

Authentic Leadership **61**

Servant Leadership **63**

5 **Developing a Leadership Practice** 67

Reexamination of Leadership Definition and Theory **67**

Leadership Goals **70**

Develop a Leadership Plan and Practice **71**

*Go Lead!* *75*

*Bibliography* *77*

# getting started

This book is a concise guide for library leaders from all types of libraries, especially those who are new to leadership and aspire to hold leadership positions. This book will help you learn about leadership, become a better leader, and develop your own leadership practice. The content of this book is not new or groundbreaking; the principles of leadership have been the same for ages. But the material is presented in a manner that requires you to engage with the content in a meaningful way. The point of this book is not to explain to you how to lead, but for you to discover why you want to lead, how you can best lead, and what your unique leadership practice looks like. For you to be an effective leader, you must first understand who you are as a leader. What do you care about as a leader? What makes you excited about leadership? For whom are you leading? Why do you want to be a leader? What values guide you as a leader? What feels most like you? Your leadership journey and practice should be guided by your curiosity about yourself and your work. What fascinates and motivates you? No one right way to lead exists. What should you do? How should you act? The answers to those questions depend on you and your library. You need to be what your library needs you to be. You need to lead how you want to be led.

Before you start your leadership journey, remember that leadership is difficult. You will worry you are not good enough to lead, but you must follow your purpose and do it anyway. When you want to quit, discover what you are afraid of and work through the fear. You will encounter critics. You cannot silence the critics, but you do not have to listen to them. Those people who are critical of your choices, are they happy with theirs? Dream big. Do big. Develop your leadership plan and follow it. Lead every day. Over time, with an unwavering belief and through hard work, your leadership self will appear. Think of leaders you admire. They struggled too. You have to love leading enough to figure it out for yourself. You have to be brave enough to try and fail. Be resilient. Do what you need to do, have to do, that makes you better. You can copy what is in the leadership literature and repeat the past, or you can create your own leadership future. Take risks. Give yourself permission to try, do, fail, and succeed. What are you depriving yourself of by not doing it? Do it your way, not some "expert's" way.

> "Leading people is the most challenging and, therefore, the most gratifying undertaking of all human endeavors."
>
> —JOCKO WILLINK

Some things are just givens for leaders. To lead successfully, you must work hard, never stop learning and growing, challenge yourself, ignore the doubt, be flexible and adaptable, see things from multiple perspectives and angles, be mindful of your actions, reflect on what you have done and how you can improve, communicate clearly and honestly, be strategic, be disciplined and courageous, and trust yourself enough to do it your own way. This book will help you develop these habits and abilities and many more by focusing on two overriding aspects of leadership: leading yourself and leading others. The essentials of leading yourself include knowing your purpose, being focused, and loving the craft. Leading others means being able to relate to others, developing a mission and vision, and modeling the way for those in the organization.

This book is intended to help you become the best leader you can by creating your own unique leadership identity and developing your own leadership practice that will allow you to make a powerful and positive impact on your library while living out your unique leadership vision. You will analyze your leadership styles, strengths, and weaknesses and create your own definition of leadership. Throughout this book, you will be asked to go back to your original work and think about how you can incorporate the information you just read into your leadership analysis and definition. By the end of the book, you will have developed your very own leadership theory and definition that you can use to guide you in your career, if you are willing to do the work, the heavy lifting, and deep thinking required for introspection, awareness, and development. By following the activities in this book and using them to inform your leadership practice, you will add value to your leadership and your library. Start today by asking yourself, "What can I do today to make myself a better leader?"

one

# Leadership Self-Analysis

Chances are if you are reading this book, you have thought about leadership. Not just that you want to become a library leader, but about the big questions like what, exactly, is leadership and what makes for a good leader? For this portion of the book, do not think about, look up, or copy what other people have said about leadership. Instead, think about what leadership means to you, how you define it, and what stands out to you about good and bad leaders. For these sections, no right or wrong answers exist. The answers you give should be the answers that you find important to you and your leadership development.

## DEFINITION OF LEADERSHIP

Before you can create your leadership style and develop your leadership practice, you must first define what you mean by leadership. The world does not lack for definitions of leadership. Seemingly every book, article, video, and seminar on leadership has its own definition. In their most broad sense, definitions of leadership are about influencing followers to achieve organizational goals, but many researchers also define leadership as helping followers reach their fullest potential, creating other leaders, developing organizational unity and success, and a whole lot more. No right or wrong definitions exist. Take some time to think about what leadership means to you. What does it mean to you to be a leader? What makes a leader successful? How do you define leadership?

**EXAMPLE** | Leadership is ethically influencing others to achieve group goals.

**Write your definition of leadership below.**

________________________________________________________

________________________________________________________

________________________________________________________

________________________________________________________

________________________________________________________

________________________________________________________

## LEADERSHIP TRAITS, SKILLS, AND ABILITIES

In order to be a good leader according to your definition of leadership, a leader will need to have certain traits, skills, and abilities. Some people are better at certain things than others, but all of these traits should be ones a person can learn, develop, and become better at. So while leaders are typically taller than the average person, tall is not a trait that can be learned and therefore should not be one of your leadership traits. Again, no right or wrong answers exist. The traits you select should be important to you and allow a leader to be successful according to your definition of leadership. What do you think are the most important traits, skills, and abilities a leader should have? Take some time to think about this section and come back to it if needed. You do not have to fill in all the blanks, but try for at least three. If you have some trouble developing a list of traits, then stop and think about people you think are good leaders. What traits and skills do they have that make them good? You can also think about some bad leaders. What do they do that make them bad, and what would it look like if those bad traits were turned to good?

**EXAMPLE** | Based on the example definition, the leader traits, skills, and abilities would include ethical, charismatic, and visionary.

Important Leadership Traits, Skills, and Abilities

1. ______________________
2. ______________________
3. ______________________
4. ______________________
5. ______________________
6. ______________________
7. ______________________
8. ______________________
9. ______________________
10. ______________________

## THEORY OF LEADERSHIP

A definition of leadership is only a small part of leadership. A good definition needs a good theory in order to connect all the moving parts of leadership and place your leadership definition and skills within a larger context. How a leader leads is wide open to interpretation, opinion, and predilection. For this exercise, a theory is how a leader would act, behave, and do in order to make the above definition of leadership a reality. For example, if you define leadership as moving an organization toward its vision, then your leadership theory would describe leaders as needing to be visionary team builders who are influential communicators and facilitate organizational transformation. Again, no right or wrong theories of leadership exist. Take some time to think about how leaders should act in the real world. The following are some questions that might help you form your leadership theory, but the theory should feel right for you. How does a leader lead? How is leadership manifested according to your definition? What should a leader be doing or not be doing in order to be a leader?

**EXAMPLE** | An "ethical influencer" is a leader who has high moral standards, a strong understanding of their own values, and the ability to relate well to others.

Write your theory of leadership below.

______________________________________________

______________________________________________

______________________________________________

## Personal Leadership SWOT Analysis

Complete a leadership SWOT analysis using your definition, traits, and theory as a guide. A SWOT analysis stands for strengths, weaknesses, opportunities, and threats. This is how people and organizations can assess where they are currently in order to better determine how to get where they want to go. A SWOT analysis is composed of internal (strengths and weaknesses), external (opportunities and threats), helpful (strengths and opportunities), and hurtful (weaknesses and threats) components. Self-analysis can be hard. We are often too critical of ourselves, magnifying our faults and diminishing the good things we do. Work hard to be honest with yourself about your strengths and weaknesses. Try not to downplay one or magnify the other. You can ask other people if you like, but this should really be about your perception of where you are right now—at this moment—on your leadership journey. Below are some questions to help you as you complete your analysis.

Using your own definition, theory, and list of traits and skills, assess your:

1. Strengths as a Leader (Internal-Helpful)

    - What advantages do you have as a leader?
    - What do you do better than anyone else?
    - What experiences have you had that others have not?
    - What do others see as your strengths?

2. Weaknesses as a Leader (Internal-Hurtful)

    - What could you improve?
    - What should you avoid?
    - What do others see as your weaknesses?

______________________________________________

______________________________________________

______________________________________________

______________________________________________

______________________________________________

______________________________________________

3. Opportunities to Practice, Learn, and Improve as a Leader (External-Helpful)

    - What opportunities are there for you to learn about leadership?
    - What opportunities are there for you to practice leadership?
    - What opportunities exist for you to try different leadership approaches to see what works?
    - What are your opportunities for reflection?
    - How can you best use these to your advantage?

______________________________________________

______________________________________________

______________________________________________

______________________________________________

______________________________________________

______________________________________________

4. Threats to Your Ability to Develop as a Leader (External-Hurtful)

   - What obstacles do you face?
   - What are others doing that could negatively affect your leadership development?
   - Are you aware of changes in leadership preferences, libraries, and the external environment? A lack of opportunities? A very big weakness? Discrimination? Reputation? Work ethic?

5. Over which of your weaknesses and threats do you have control? How can you go about turning those threats over which you have control into opportunities? Forging your weaknesses into strengths? Forget about those over which you have no control and concentrate on ways you can become the best leader you can.

## UNIQUE SELLING PROPOSITION

For this final piece of self-analysis, write your leadership unique selling proposition or USP. A USP is a way companies and individuals separate themselves from the competition. It answers the basic questions of what makes this option better than all the rest and why that is important. What differentiates you from other library leaders? Why should someone chose to follow you over another potential leader? In order to write an effective USP, you should know what your potential followers value, rank yourself by these values, use your SWOT analysis to know what you are good at, and emphasize the areas in which you really excel. Another way to look at your USP is your leadership slogan. In that way, it should be short and to the point.

**EXAMPLE** | I am a leader who makes the right decisions the right way. Or, I imbue the library with a sense of ethics, transparency, and responsibility by modeling those qualities in all of my work and behavior.

**Write your leadership USP below.**

________________________________________

________________________________________

________________________________________

________________________________________

________________________________________

________________________________________

________________________________________

________________________________________

> Ego gives us confidence, ambition, and the determination to move forward. Ego also makes us put ourselves above the library, think we are too good for a job, and believe we are the reason for it all. Effective leaders keep their ego in check.

## LEADERSHIP AMBITION

Now, let's put it all together. Use your leadership definition, traits, strengths, weaknesses, and unique values and approach to decide who you want to be as a leader. What kind of leader do you want to be? Do not answer a "good one." Be ambitious. This is your leadership ambition after all. In one sentence, what is your ultimate, no-holds-barred, no self-censoring aspiration as a leader? Do you want to be the Librarian of Congress? Do you want to be a powerful transformational leader who ushers in the new age of librarianship? Do you want to be known for your human touch and ability to relate to others? How about mentoring and developing underrepresented groups as leaders? Or do you want to be known as an innovative leader who moved every library you led toward living their vision?

Write just one sentence below.

two

# Leadership, Followership, and Organizational Culture

Leadership is an important and powerful force in an organization, but it is only one of several forces that make up organizational life. The other forces that operate within and on the organization are followers and organizational culture. Followers act on and act out the organization's mission and vision. Followers perform the organization's frontline work, and they can either make a leader look golden or thwart and stymie the leader at every turn. Organizational culture is the unique way organizational members see and interact with the world. Culture dictates how and what work is done in an organization, and it dictates not only how leaders and followers act but also who can be a part of the organization. Each one of these parts influences and is influenced by the other two. Unfortunately, most leadership books and literature focus only on leadership and ignore the roles followers and culture play. This chapter will introduce each of these forces and what roles they play in an organization, leaving a more detailed discussion on leadership theory, which includes followers, for chapter four.

## LEADERSHIP

Ralph Stogdill, an organizational researcher and theorist, defined leadership this way: "Leadership may be considered as the process (act) of influencing the activities of an organized group in its efforts toward goal setting and goal achievement." Stogdill wrote this definition in 1953, and over the years the thinking about leadership has evolved. In the early 1980s, Linda Smircich and Gareth Morgan developed a now famous and frequently used leadership definition: "Leadership is the process whereby one or more individuals succeeds in attempting to frame and define the reality of others." A simplified version of that definition is leadership is about creating and managing meaning in the organization. Humans are meaning-making creatures, and we want to belong to something bigger than ourselves and live with and work toward a greater purpose. This definition of leadership as meaning making came in to use because, by the early 1980s, modern organizations and modern work had lost much of its meaning. Work became transactions done via networked connections in pursuit of company profit, and many employees began to feel cut off from any meaning in their work. This was made all the worse when those employees were "downsized," replaced by computers and algorithms. Leaders as meaning makers sounds pretty fancy, but what that really means for a library is mission plus vision. This combination gives the library's work meaning, helps inform decision making, and allows leaders to manage and frame events.

No matter how you define it, leadership is about influencing people (followers) to complete work (mission) that moves the organization toward meeting its goals (vision). Stogdill's definition of leadership makes this explicit, while Smircich and Morgan's definition emphasizes the why of organizational work—the importance of the work being done—as the way to influence followers. Leaders influence followers to not only do what is best for the organization but also to want to do what is best for the organization. Leaders must align organizational goals, values, and work with followers' goals, values, and work in order to make what is best for the organization the best for followers as well. Everything a leader does—good or bad—has an influence on the organization both in the present and in the future.

Now, let's try an experiment. Take any definition of leadership—it can be your definition you created in chapter one, Smircich and Morgan's, Stogdill's, or any of the many definitions of leadership available—and replace the word "leadership" in that definition with any number of organizational terms: "mission," "culture," "structure," "work," etc. Does the definition still work and make sense? Let's try it using Stogdill's definition above.

> Leadership may be considered as the process (act) of influencing the activities of an organized group in its efforts toward goal setting and goal achievement.

Let's replace "leadership" with "organizational culture."

> Organizational culture may be considered as the process (act) of influencing the activities of an organized group in its efforts toward goal setting and goal achievement.

Does that definition work? Does it make sense? Is it true for organizational life? Yes, yes, and yes. This tells us there is more to organizations than just leadership. Leaders are not the be-all and end-all when it comes to organizational success and failure, but one would have a hard time learning that in the leadership literature, which mostly spotlights the difference leaders—and only leaders—make. The almost single-minded focus on leadership in organizational life has led to the "romance of leadership." This romance is the exaggeration of what leaders can do and the role they play in an organization. The romance of leadership creates the vastly overinflated expectations that followers have of leaders. These unrealistic expectations of leaders not only contribute to the failure of good leaders but also to fewer qualified people who are willing to become leaders.

> As a leader, you have a limited amount of "leadership capital." Make sure you spend it wisely on things that truly matter and are of great importance.

This romance also establishes an unfair distribution of credit and blame for organizational successes and failures. Some research shows that leaders receive over 50 percent of the credit and the blame for organizational outcomes, but leaders account for less than 15 percent of those outcomes. We are meaning-making creatures. We want to find a reason why a project turned out well or ended poorly so we can replicate the success or fix the problem. Organizations, though, are very complex. Even a small library is composed of many moving parts: librarians, library staff, and student workers or volunteers interacting with faculty, staff, alumni, and/or community patrons. All of these individuals bring to these interactions their lives up that point. A bad breakfast, a fight with a spouse, or a child failing algebra can all impact how any one of these individuals interacts with another. All the work, planning, and effort that go into a typical project, and its success or failure, can come down to someone's mood at one particular moment in time. Good leaders take responsibility for all that happens in their library, but they are also keenly aware that they are one piece of the organizational leadership puzzle. Leadership consists of interactions between leaders and followers within a unique organizational culture. In these interactions, leaders communicate, followers interpret and act, and culture controls how and what a leader communicates and how followers interpret and take action.

Think about a time when you failed to show effective leadership. What could you have done differently?

How has the romance of leadership affected you as either a leader or a follower?

How does your leadership theory and definition overcome the "problem of substitution" and differentiate the effect of leadership from the effect of the library's culture, mission, or other aspects? How would you change your theory and definition so that it does?

## FOLLOWERSHIP

Earlier in this book, we discussed definitions of leadership and even wrote our own. Those definitions include influencing, vision, and goal achievement, but what they typically do not include are the people being influenced, buying into the vision, and achieving the goals: followers. "Followers" is a loaded term. Some people find negative connotation in the word, thinking it implies an uncritical, unthinking, mindlessness. In this book, the term "followers" is value neutral. If leaders create meaning, then followers make that meaning into reality. Before that can happen, though, followers must accept the meaning being created by leaders. This is far from easy, especially in a profession like librarianship. People become librarians for many different reasons, with just as many expectations of what their work will be like and consist of.

Followers make meaning a reality by acting on the meaning being created. They do the work of the mission to take the library toward its vision. This action requires interpretation. Sometimes these interpretations are accurate and beneficial, and other times they are inaccurate and hurtful. Once in a while, interpretations are intentionally sabotaging. Much of leadership is about the actions and perceptions of followers. Whether a leader possesses certain traits, skills, and abilities and whether that leader is any good as a leader is determined by the perception of followers. Those perceptions depend on context, culture, situation, and organization. Followers play an enormous part in any organization and are a powerful force. In fact, it may well be that followers teach leadership to leaders.

The romance of leadership, however, understates the power followers have, if they are even mentioned. The leadership literature tends to think of followers as inert pieces that are moved by and acted upon by leaders. But nothing could be further from the truth. Without the action of followers, an organization will not be able to accomplish even the most basic of goals. Without the approval and buy-in of followers, a leader will never be successful. This is what makes the ability to relate to other people, to communicate with them, to understand them, and to help them move toward a future state so important to leadership. Even in the most top-down authoritarian workplaces, leaders who cannot relate to others and build relationships are doomed to failure. Whether through aggressive, passive, or passive-aggressive means, followers will win out. Followers have a lot of power, and it is a leader's job to help guide the use of that power in ways that help the organization accomplish its mission. The interaction of leaders, followers, and meaning is where leadership takes place. Leadership is not how a leader will make an organization better, which is the romance of leadership, but how leaders and followers work together for organizational success. It is critical to remember, however, that leaders and followers operate in a unique environment with its own culture and established norms of being and doing.

Have you ever witnessed a leader unable to influence followers? What do you think lay at the root of that leader's inability to influence?

How does your definition and theory of leadership account for followers?

## ORGANIZATIONAL CULTURE

Leaders and followers are limited in how they can act and what they can do by the norms of the organization's culture. In essence, everyone in an organization is playing a role, either that of follower or leader. When either followers or leaders act outside of their culturally prescribed behavior, they can face harsh rebuke from others in the culture. This means that everyone in a culture must meet certain sets of standards for behavior, skills, traits, abilities, and how they view the world and the work they are doing. Those leaders and followers who cannot or will not fit within the cultural expectations do not last long in the organization. Those who are selected as leaders, and perhaps more importantly who are successful as leaders, are a cultural prototype and model of the norms of behavior. This is one of the main reasons "modeling the way" is so important for leaders. Culture then plays an enormous role in not only how we act, but also how we perceive the world around us.

> Balance who you are as a person—your unique way of doing leadership—with your library's cultural expectations of leadership.

Organizational culture starts with an organization's founders and their values. As more people adopt these cultural values, the culture becomes stronger. Those organizational members who for whatever reason do not adopt the same values leave the organization. Over time, this creates a strong and homogenous cultural belief system. As new members are added to the organization—including leaders—they are selected according to how well they meet the cultural norms, and with each new generation of organizational members, the culture grows even stronger. Organizational culture becomes so strong that eventually people will self-select to which organizations they will apply based on culture.

What is organizational culture? Organizational culture can be categorized and defined by types: clan, adhocracy, market, hierarchical, communal, mercenary, fragmented, networked, or bureaucratic (Cameron and Quinn 2011). But this approach only provides a partial and superficial understanding of organizational culture. Organizational culture was best defined by Edgar Schein, who called it

> a pattern of shared basic assumptions that was learned by a group as it solved its problems of external adaptation and internal integration, that has worked well enough to be considered valid and, therefore, to be taught to new members as the correct way to perceive, think, and feel in relation to those problems (Schein 2004, 17).

Another way to define culture is "This is how we do things around here." It is how people perceive, think, and feel. Culture is accepted norms of behavior around everything from how one dresses at work to the type of work performed to how that work should be done. Organizational culture can be understood by answering the question, "What does it mean to be a part of this organization?" (Taylor 2017). Influencing followers is done by a leader emphasizing values. Those same values are what spur or stop followers from taking action. And, of course, it is values that are the foundation of organizational culture, which means culture plays an outsized role in organizational work. Many, however, are not even aware culture exists. They simply know this is how it has always been done. Real cultural change, changing the way people behave and express their culture, is long and difficult. What makes it even more difficult is culture itself is providing the greatest resistance.

Have you ever experienced organizational culture thwarting needed change from happening, stopping the implementation of a good idea, or encouraging dysfunctional or maladaptive behavior?

How does your definition and theory of leadership account for organizational culture?

Thinking of your library, how would you describe its culture? How is the culture conducive to leadership? How does it hinder leadership?

## THE LEADERSHIP/FOLLOWERSHIP PROCESS

The Leadership/Followership Process takes into account the three main factors of organizational life: leaders, followers, and organizational culture. When we talk of leadership, we must also talk of followership and organizational culture. All three influence and are influenced by the other two. Leadership occurs in the interaction between followers and leaders. These interactions consist of meaning creation by leaders and acceptance, interpretation, and action by followers. These interactions occur within a unique culture that influences and constrains every part of these interactions, including how, when, where, and why these interactions occur. Leaders use meaning to attract and influence followers by defining what work is important and how it is meaningful. Meaning gives purpose to the work performed and guides decision making. Meaning comes from the library's vision and mission, but it is also tightly controlled by the library's culture. Followers manifest the meaning through the work they perform, but how the work is performed is also strongly influenced by the organizational culture.

None of these parts, however, are static. All are dynamic. They each influence and are influenced by the other two. Figure 2.1 is a graphic representation of this dynamic. As followers and leaders learn the organizational culture and teach it to new members, room exists for a reinterpretation of the culture,

FIGURE 2.1

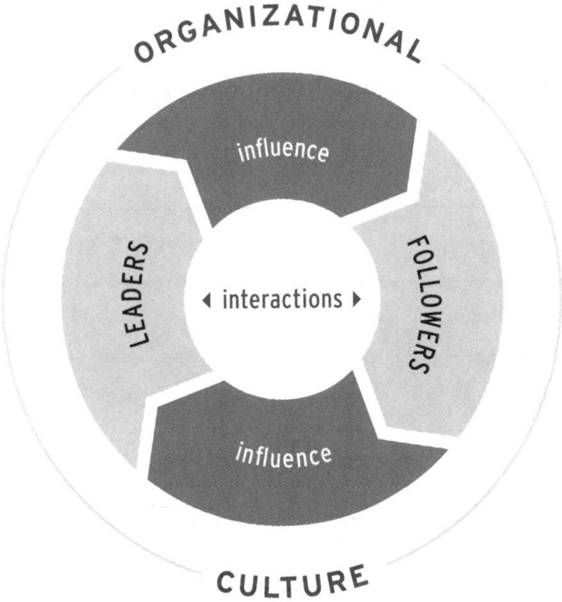


Tayler Brooke Webb

thereby changing the organizational culture. As stated earlier, organizational culture flows from an organization's values. Those values become stronger over time as leaders and followers model, follow, and reinforce them. But this does not mean those values cannot change over time. While not an easy process, leaders can use their influence to create meaning around the adoption of new values and the discarding of old values that no longer serve the organization. If enough followers choose to accept these new values, then the organizational culture will begin to change. Here is where a leader's organizational awareness of the library's politics, cliques, and influencers becomes crucial. A leader must be able to sway the library's informal leaders to adopt and spread the new cultural values. Followers' acceptance of new values will depend at least in part on how they perceive the values to benefit the work they do and if they will be rewarded for adopting these new values. Their acceptance also depends on the level of trust and their perception of the library leader. Once a tipping point has been reached, followers begin to influence each other, making the new values the norm by which organizational members are expected to adhere. These new values reshape the organization's culture, and this changed culture influences leader/follower interactions. Followers can also introduce and adopt new values that change the organizational culture, even if leadership is not in favor of these new values. In this scenario, leader/follower interactions could be influenced to such a degree that the current leadership is removed (Martin 2019).

## YOUR LEADERSHIP EXPERIENCE

What is your leadership experience? What have you found to be true and not true about being a leader?

How does your definition and theory of leadership add value to the library it could not otherwise get from other aspects of the organization?

Have confidence in the value you bring as a leader. It is what separates you from everyone else.

three

# Leading Yourself

What it takes to be a successful leader is the same as it takes to be successful in any other area of your personal or work life: purpose, focus, and love of the craft. The how (mission) leads to the what (vision), and both are supported by the why (purpose). With a strong enough why, any what can be reached by various means of how, but it all flows from the why. All three of these parts reinforce, lead to, and support the other two parts. In this chapter, you will explore your leadership purpose—why you are a leader. This purpose is what helps you be an original leader, and originality brings value. Your purpose allows you to move and work in a way natural to you and be guided by what is demanded of you. Focus is vitally important for any leader and is needed in every facet of leadership—from focus on the work right in front of you to focus on the strategic picture of your library. Here, we use "focus" to mean your focus on your mission and vision as a leader. Growing out of your purpose, your mission and vision are what you want to do and where you want to go as a leader. This focus on your mission and vision helps keep you grounded in who you are and keeps you from jumping from one thing to another without any real direction. Finally, we will explore your love of leadership and librarianship. You cannot lead it if you do not love it. All three of these things form your essence as a leader and are nurtured by your honesty and sincerity. For good measure, we will also discuss self-care as a leader and how important it is for you as a library leader to take care of yourself to prevent burnout, poor health, and bad habits.

## LEADING YOURSELF EFFECTIVELY

### Purpose

A leader must have a purpose for leading, a reason why he/she wants to lead. The foundation of any purpose is values. So in order to be successful, a leader must not just state a purpose, or have a purpose, but must embody that purpose every day. A leader's sense of purpose is what guides, motivates, and informs all decisions. A purpose is both a guide and a support system for a leader. When faced with a plethora of choices, a purpose helps a leader decide which one to follow. Purpose also supports a leader on their journey. It acts as the why, helping a leader to carry on when he/she no longer feels like carrying on. A strong purpose helps a leader from becoming lost in a sea of options and allows a leader to know what they should and should not be doing. A leadership purpose allows a leader to let go of affectation and fear. A purpose is who a leader is. Often leaders get caught up in trying not to look foolish or dumb. Leaders want to make good choices and avoid bad choices, but, to be truly effective, leaders must move in the way their purpose dictates. Leaders should never apologize for or be embarrassed about being who they are as a leader and living their leadership purpose. A purpose also allows you to know if you are working in the right organization and environment for you. Moving against your purpose and acting counter to your values will cause you to be in a chronic state of stress, which will have a terrible effect on your health. Working counter to your purpose will also cause you to lower your standards and accept less of yourself and others around you, making you less effective as a leader. Not only does a purpose allow you to know yourself better and make the right choices for yourself, but it also lets others understand you and know what you and your work are about. By knowing you better, followers can trust you more and work more easily with you.

**Be known for something positive**

*Your Attitude*
*Your Values*
*Your Vision*
*Your Hard Work*
*Your Expertise*
*Your Influence*

As was mentioned earlier, a purpose has as its foundation your personal and professional values. Take some time to think about your values and list them below. For some, this may take little time, but others may need to spend some time really thinking about and formulating their values and belief system. You do not have to fill in all the blanks, but try for at least five in both categories.

Personal Values

1. ____________________ 6. ____________________

2. ____________________ 7. ____________________

3. ____________________ 8. ____________________

4. ____________________ 9. ____________________

5. ____________________ 10. ____________________

Professional Values

1. ____________________ 6. ____________________

2. ____________________ 7. ____________________

3. ____________________ 8. ____________________

4. ____________________ 9. ____________________

5. ____________________ 10. ____________________

Are any of your personal values in conflict? Professional values? How could you rectify this?

Now, take some time to think about why you want to be a leader. What is it about leading a library that attracts you? Why do you feel the need to lead?

Using what you have written in the above exercises, take some time to develop your leadership purpose. Remember, this purpose is composed of your values and what attracts you to leadership in the first place. Your purpose is why you want to lead. It is your motivation for showing up every day and doing the work that needs to be done, even when it would be easier to do anything else.

What is your leadership purpose?

## Focus

Focus makes the difference between average and good, good and great. A successful leader must have focus. A leader must minimize distractions and be focused on the library's day-to-day work in order to oversee projects, track budgets, and complete reports on time. This, of course, is in addition to the myriad other duties of a library leader, the numerous meetings, and developing donors. A leader needs to have focus on what needs to be accomplished now and what is coming due in the very near future. But a leader must also be focused on the big picture, not just the tactical but the strategic too. In order to lead yourself successfully, you must know and be focused on your leadership mission and vision. Without the focus on what work you want to do and where you want to go as a leader, you will never get anywhere as a leader. This requires you to balance your inner (leadership mission and vision) and outer (library mission and vision) focus. Your leadership mission and vision grow out of your leadership purpose. Your purpose is your overarching "why" of being a leader, your vision is where you want to go on your leadership journey, and your mission is the work you need to be doing to both satisfy your purpose and reach your vision. Focus allows you to know what work to do to reach your vision but also what work not to do, which can be even more important.

Before you develop your leadership mission and vision, take a few minutes to honestly assess your focus. How focused are you? On a scale of 1–10, rate your focus.

1 2 3 4 5 6 7 8 9 10

How can you improve your focus? What are some of your major distractions? How can you lessen them or get rid of them altogether?

Do you delegate well? **Y / N** Distractions can take the form of work others should be doing. By delegating, we free ourselves to focus on our library's priorities.

Now, think about where you want to go as a leader. What is your leadership endgame? Where do you hope to be or who do you want to be as a leader? That is your leadership vision. This might be similar to your leadership ambition, but not the same thing. Your ambition might be to be the Librarian of Congress or the director of a large public library, but your vision might be to develop a library culture that embraces all aspects of ethical leadership and ethical decision making.

What is your leadership vision?

________________________________________

________________________________________

________________________________________

________________________________________

________________________________________

________________________________________

Are there any special skills you will need to develop or training you will need to complete to reach your vision? Would a mentor help you?

________________________________________

________________________________________

________________________________________

________________________________________

________________________________________

________________________________________

For your mission, think about what you can start doing now to reach your vision. What kinds of work should you be doing to successfully reach your vision? This will change over time as you get closer to your vision or as you refine your vision. But for now, take some to think about your mission. Perhaps your mission might be to develop a strong understanding of your values to better inform your ethical leadership, to practice ethical leadership as a library department head, and to spread the word of ethical leadership through publishing and presenting.

What is your leadership mission?

______________________________________________

______________________________________________

______________________________________________

______________________________________________

______________________________________________

______________________________________________

## The Love of the Craft

If you do not love it, then you cannot lead it. You cannot inspire others unless you are inspired. People will know when you are faking it. Without love of the work, you will never be truly inspired. In order to be a successful library leader, you must be good at and enjoy the work of being both a leader and a librarian. No one is born good at either; everyone can learn to be good at both. And if you are good at something and enjoy it, then why would you not want to do it? You can be good at leadership and/or librarianship but not enjoy it. This will only take you so far. You can do well, but you will be limited in what you can accomplish. You can also enjoy leadership and/or librarianship but be bad at it. In this scenario, you will accomplish nothing. The true nexus of great work is to be both good at it and enjoy it.

Along with your competence and enjoyment comes confidence. No one can give you confidence or self-esteem or the ability to make a decision. You can learn how to do just about everything, but you cannot learn these things. You either have to fake it until you make it, jump right in, or find something else to do. No one will follow a leader who has no confidence. You do not have to have all the answers, but you have to ensure others you have the ability to find the answers and use them. It is okay to be unsure, to be nervous, to not know. It is not okay to be a disaster who is constantly falling apart. If you cannot hold yourself together, then how will others trust you to hold the library together?

**Give, Not Take**

In order to add value to your library and have a positive influence on everyone you meet, be a giver instead of a taker.

Ask yourself:

- What can I do for the library?
- How can I help those in the library?

What do you like about leadership and why?

______________________________

______________________________

______________________________

______________________________

______________________________

______________________________

What do you dislike about leadership and why?

______________________________

______________________________

______________________________

______________________________

______________________________

______________________________

______________________________

What do you like about librarianship and why?

______________________________________________

______________________________________________

______________________________________________

______________________________________________

______________________________________________

______________________________________________

What do you dislike about librarianship and why?

______________________________________________

______________________________________________

______________________________________________

______________________________________________

______________________________________________

______________________________________________

Looking over your answers to the above exercises, do you think you have the kind of love and dedication to the craft that is needed to be a great library leader?

______________________________________________

______________________________________________

______________________________________________

______________________________________________

______________________________________________

## SELF-CARE

"Godfather of Soul" James Brown "paid the cost to be the boss," and so must you. Being a leader is difficult. It can be mentally, emotionally, and even physically draining. While purpose, focus, and love of the craft are indispensable to a successful library leader, self-care is invaluable. As a leader, you must take the time to care for and support yourself. If you do not take care of your health, then no one else will. And as a leader, if you are not healthy, then you will not be successful. Self-care comes in many forms, and below are some major areas. Please note: using alcohol or drugs, eating sugary and fatty foods, and doing other negative activities are not healthy ways to deal with stress and are not self-care. Engaging in such activities can lead to addiction and serious health problems. Please seek help if you are dependent on alcohol, drugs, or other negative activities.

> "In your actions, don't procrastinate. In your conversations, don't confuse. In your thoughts, don't wander. In your soul, don't be passive or aggressive. In your life, don't be all about business."
>
> —MARCUS AURELIUS

### Digital Disconnect

In today's ever-connected, always-on world, it is critical for leaders to be able to disconnect from digital devices and computers. This can include setting a time each day when you no longer check or use your devices or a day once a week or month when you do not use any devices for the entire day. Of course, this is difficult for leaders to do in a world that expects them to be connected all day, every day. But you must make some time when you are free from your devices and the work they bring.

What is your plan for digital disconnect? Will you take an entire day away from your devices? Or set a time each day when you will no longer look at and use them?

________________________________________

________________________________________

________________________________________

________________________________________

## Mental Rejuvenation

Find a hobby or activity that you can do outside of work that allows you to recharge your battery. No matter how much you love what you do, you need time away from the work. These activities can include exercise, yoga, gardening, surfing, nonwork-related reading, and a host of other activities that allow you to decompress, challenge yourself in a different way from your work, and/or scratch an itch.

What activities provide you mental rejuvenation, that you do simply for the joy of doing them? When will you make time for them in your schedule?

## Be Kind to Yourself

We are all our own worst critics. Show yourself self-compassion. Forgive yourself for your mistakes and stop beating yourself up over what you did in the past. Being kind to yourself also involves finding healthy ways to deal with stress.

How will you healthily deal with the stress of being a leader?

## Strive for Balance

We will rarely, if ever, have a perfect work-life balance. Sometimes work takes over, and sometimes life takes over. Instead, strive for the kind of balance that is found in nature and not let one plant in your garden become too overgrown. Plant a variety of plants and keep them all well-maintained.

What does life balance look like for you?

How will you know when your life is no longer in balance and needs some readjusting?

## Self-Identity

How do you define yourself? Are you other things than a library leader? By defining yourself outside of your job, you will have a better work-life balance and know when it is time to step aside as a leader.

How do you define yourself? Is this helpful or hurtful to your self-care?

What other forms of self-care do you practice?

How can you be better at practicing self-care?

______________________________________________

______________________________________________

______________________________________________

______________________________________________

______________________________________________

______________________________________________

**Mindfulness**

Mindfulness makes for better library leaders. Mindfulness is a form of self-care and makes us more aware when we are out of balance. It improves self-awareness as well as awareness of others and our environment. Here is a quick and easy mindfulness practice:

- Place your hand on your belly button and take a deep breath. This should push your belly and hand out.
- Hold the breath for a beat and then exhale, leaving your hand where it is.
- As you take more deep breaths, make sure to touch your belly button to your hand.
- Do this for ten breaths, once or several times each day.

four

# Leading Others

Leadership styles, theories, and philosophies can be limiting. What works well in one setting might not work in another. What works well with one type of behavior or a certain kind of person does not work well with others. Leaders must be flexible. A good library leader should not follow a set pattern of leading but use the various leadership patterns as a guide in creating a unique leadership image. This does not make leadership definitions and theories useless, however. Leadership is a lot more complicated than the leadership literature lets on, but at the same time a lot simpler too. Leaders are better off sticking to core principles of leadership, knowing their strengths and weaknesses, borrowing from theories what works for them and their organization, and being in a constant state of learning. As you read over these leadership styles, theories, and philosophies, take away what works for you and leave the rest behind. Before you explore some major theories of leadership below, you must first learn the three basic elements of leading followers: relating to others, mission and vision, and modeling the way.

## LEADING OTHERS EFFECTIVELY

### Relating to Others

As a leader, you must be able to relate to and work with all types and various kinds of people. You need to make human connections with people of your library. This means recognizing them as people and allowing them to be heard and express their thoughts and emotions. Relationships are a big part of leadership, no matter the setting (Martin 2017). This is difficult to do, however. Relationships are a two-way street and require the participation of both parties. A follower may not want to develop a relationship with you out of a lack of trust. Trust is difficult to build and easy to lose. To gain trust, you need to use your self-awareness and self-management—two important pieces of emotional intelligence discussed below—to monitor and control your behavior, attitude, and communication. You need to be consistent in both your actions and your words and display no hypocrisy between the two. As a leader, you need to be able to speak and act both intellectually and emotionally. This allows others in the library to feel your warmth and energy, to know that you care, and to recognize you are human too.

Being able to relate well to others also means being able to successfully resolve conflict. As a leader, you need to choose your battles wisely. Sometimes you have to absorb problems, and other times you need to let those involved solve it for themselves. Discerning when to act and when not to act requires experience, understanding of the people involved and the situation, and a bit of wisdom. But when you do decide to confront a situation, work toward finding a solution. The optimal solution is win/win, but this is not always possible. Sometimes the resolution of conflicts involves a win/lose resolution. These situations require great skill and tact. Any circumstance involving winners also involves losers. Being in a win/lose mindset creates unnecessary tension because whoever did not "win" is a "loser." After enough losses by your followers, you will start to think you are surrounded by losers, who, by the way, are sore and would love revenge on you. When working to resolve conflict, adopt as minimal an attitude of moral superiority as needed. Because even if you did win, nobody likes a poor winner. This is why leaders need to keep their ego in check and focus on what is best for the organization. Never pull rank and never follow a course of action that cannot be undone, especially when it comes to something you might say in the heat of the moment.

To be a successful relations leader who is also able to move the library toward its vision, you need to develop a "people first, mission always" mindset. This means always focusing on the library's being successful in its mission and moving toward its vision, but at the same time taking care, supporting, and connecting with the people in the organization. This requires the use of both empathy and compassion. Several types of empathy exist, but, at its most basic level, empathy means being aware of others' emotions and the organization's emotions. Compassion means recognizing when people are suffering and acting to help them relieve their suffering. For a library leader, this could mean recognizing and helping those in the organization who are struggling with their work, feel unheard, or lack a sense of belonging. It can also mean knowing what someone wants to achieve and supporting them. As a leader, you need to understand the people you are leading—their wants, needs, and goals—and support them at the level they need to be supported. So much of leadership is about guiding and supporting disparate people to work toward goals. These people, of course, also have wants, needs, and goals of their own. As a leader, you have to want the best for them in order to get the best from them. You also need to use your awareness to know when your team needs a break. You can run a car engine in the red for a short time, but run the engine too long in the red and it will stop working. The same holds true for people. As a leader, you may be able to run for longer in the red and on less rest than others, but you cannot expect everyone to move at your pace. Recognize when those in your library need a break and give it to them.

What are some things a leader can do to build a "people first, mission always" mindset?

How well do you relate to others? How could you improve? Are you an introvert? Too much of an extravert? Bad with names?

## Mission and Vision

To be a leader, you have to know where you are going and you have to know where the organization is going. In order to be successful, a vision must be shared. The best way to share a vision is to build it from the ground up. Get everyone's input and have the library build the vision together. Too often, leaders try to implement a vision from the top down. This may be seen as an "authoritarian" move leading to resentment and pushback against the vision. This, of course, makes it that much more difficult to develop the needed buy-in from followers. By working from the bottom up, everyone in the library feels as if they have had a part in shaping the library's vision and future direction. Not only does this make sharing a vision easier, but multiple perspectives and viewpoints create a stronger vision for the library.

When it comes to implementing the vision, think big, work small. As a leader, you should never underestimate the importance of small things because small things add up to big things. You just need to make sure you are focusing on the right small things and not useless minutiae. Bring the library's vision down to the library's day-to-day work, service, and programs. Not only does this make it easier to achieve the vision, but it also allows the library to see what work and activities no longer serve the library and its community, making it easier to alter or stop that work. When trying to implement a vision and move the library toward its future, start with what you have power over and can affect right now. As you have success, what and who you can influence increase in an ever-widening circle. Improvement can also come from bad steps. Never be afraid to make mistakes when working toward a goal. The list of mistakes we cannot recover from is very small. In starting a new leadership position or during rocky times in your current library, consider a realignment or a revision instead of a complete overhaul of the mission and vision. Complete overhauls take a lot time and can lead to a lot of stress and anxiety in the library, putting your new start in jeopardy or making a bad time even worse.

### Meet Hardness with Softness

When two hard objects strike each other, one or both will likely break. When hardness is met with softness, both objects survive because the blow is lessened. Do not reciprocate negative emotions or behaviors. This only makes the situation worse. Use positive emotions and behaviors to influence the other person and redirect their behavior.

Once the library's vision is created and shared and a plan is in place to move the library forward, you as a leader must be a true believer. You must do the things you need to do and do it with joy. Once you stop believing in the mission, then you need to step aside as a leader. Without your enthusiastic support, buy-in will dwindle throughout the library and forward momentum will be lost. Leaders must focus on the mission, not personal gain and ego fulfillment. Your first priority as a leader should be doing what is best for the library. A strong mission and vision are critical for all organizations, including libraries. Without a mission, vision, and the meaning they bring to the organization and its work, the library will lack focus and be more prone to a negative organizational climate.

> Celebrate the work of the library. Recognize milestones and personnel achievements.

What vision do you have for your library?

______________________________

______________________________

______________________________

______________________________

______________________________

______________________________

What steps would you take to build a shared vision throughout the library? How would you guide the process of creating a vision? Make sure everyone's voice is heard?

______________________________

______________________________

______________________________

______________________________

______________________________

______________________________

## Modeling the Way

Some days as a leader, it may seem like no one is watching you or listening to a word you say, but they most certainly are. In a study of baboons, the members of the congress looked up at the alpha baboon every 20 to 30 seconds. People pay close attention to the attitude, behavior, and work of leaders. This is why library leaders must model the way for library members. "Modeling the way" includes several pieces. One is to model good organizational behavior. This means being a model of the norms, values, and behaviors of the library's organizational culture. Leaders are expected to be prototypes of the organizational culture, and when a leader drifts too far away from the accepted behavior of the culture, the organization no longer sees the leader as "one of us" and loses trust in that leader. But, as a leader, you can also influence the library's culture by modeling the types of actions and values you want to see—or see more of—in the library.

Leaders also model the way to the library's vision. The vision is the future of the library, the end state you want as a leader. To get there, the library will have to move in a particular direction, undertake certain work and services, and stop performing others. By the work you perform as a leader and by what you reward, you are modeling how librarians and library staff should be working in the library. You are modeling the path to the vision. This is only effective when you have a shared vision. Without the shared vision, your efforts of modeling the way fall on untilled land and will not properly root, grow, and blossom. As a leader, you are modeling how to interact in the library in ways that create happiness, success, and healthy working relationships and how to work and move toward the library's shared future.

### Developing a Vision

To become better at visioning, you must first stop self-censoring. Think of as many possibilities as you can, regardless of practicality. Stay away from binary thinking like good/bad, affordable/expensive, or doable/unachievable. Develop ideas without judgment and attachment and see what comes of them and where you can go with them.

What do you model in your day-to-day workplace behavior?

___

___

___

_______________

_______________

_______________

What do you do well in your modeling? Where could you improve?

_______________

_______________

_______________

_______________

_______________

_______________

## LEADERSHIP TRAITS, SKILLS, AND ABILITIES

The study of leadership began with the study of traits. Researchers were searching for what differentiated leaders from followers. Traits were seen as innate. Great leaders were born that way because they possessed a certain kind and number of personality traits. Researchers found that leaders had greater intelligence, self-confidence, social ability, and a host of other traits than followers. This line of research suffered from several problems. One was many of the traits could not be learned. They were personality traits one developed at an early age or not at all. The second problem was no definitive list was ever developed. Many of the lists had a few traits in common—mainly the ones listed above—but also included traits like alertness, dominance, and masculinity. The research and its findings were subjective based on what one thought a successful leader should be. Traits were also found to be situational. What worked for one leader in a particular setting might not work for that leader in a very different environment.

Leadership researchers have also examined leadership skills, abilities, and styles. This line of research was mostly concerned with what leaders should know how to do. Leadership skills fell into three overarching categories: technical, human, and conceptual. A leader's technical skills are demonstrated in how well they know the work of the organization and the profession. Just about every great business leader was an expert at the work the organization did, and very many of them worked their way up the organizational ladder. Being an expert in organizational work is extremely important for a leader, mostly because it allows them to gain the trust of followers performing the day-to-day work. Human skills are how well leaders can work with people. This skill is vital because leadership is about relationships. Conceptual skills are how well leaders work with ideas. Leaders are decision makers and must decide where the organization should be dedicating its time and resources. Leaders are also responsible for the organization's mission and vision. These activities require a leader to be able to work with ideas in various forms. Leader styles are similarly broken into task—managing the structure and work of the organization to achieve goals—and relationship—dealing with people. These skills are situational and subjective, much like the research on traits, and many traits and skills overlap.

In a recent study, academic librarians were asked to think of a past library leader who had a positive impact on their daily work lives and list three characteristics of that person (Martin 2018b). They were then asked to think of what characteristics future library leaders would need to have a positive impact on the daily work lives of librarians. The two sets of results had five common traits: inter- and intrapersonal skills, communicating, having a vision, facilitating change, and being a competent and experienced librarian. These results fall within the three main skills categories of technical (competent and experienced librarian), human (inter- and intrapersonal skills and communicating), and conceptual (visioning and change agent). They also match up well with the research literature on library leaders.

**Be Approachable**

Do not lock yourself away in your office. Get out. Be seen. Be heard. Listen.

## Inter- and Intrapersonal Skills

Above all, a good library leader needs to be able to understand, care about, and have relationships with everyone in the library. This means being able to use empathy to understand the library's culture and politics, having compassion to help those in the library become better, and using self-awareness to understand their strengths and weaknesses. Library leaders with strong inter- and intrapersonal skills know when to push forward and when to ease back.

### Communicating

A good communicator listens well and listens first and communicates, both verbally and written, often and honestly. People want to feel they are being heard and their thoughts matter. They also want to be in the know about the current and projected future state of the library.

### Vision

A library needs to be moving forward, toward the future, and not be stuck in the present and looking back at the past. A visionary leader thinks about the present and plans for the future, anticipates future needs, and knows not only where the library is in the big picture but also how to successfully maneuver the library into a more advantageous position.

### Change Agent

It is a cliché at this point, but constant change is the new normal for libraries. A library leader must be able to facilitate change, which goes well beyond project management. A good change agent always puts people first. They are able to sell the people in the library on the needed change, take into account their mindset (Are they ready for more change?), celebrate the work done, and support people's transitions into the unknown work that change brings.

### Competent and Experienced Librarian

A good library leader needs to know the work of the library. Competence in an area of librarianship does not translate to good leadership, but all good library leaders need to know the work of their library in order to understand what the library does and how all the parts work together. Being a competent librarian also helps a leader from outside the library become more quickly accepted into the culture.

**Values**

Leadership skills will make you an effectual, competent leader. What makes you a good leader are your values and using those values to make difficult organizational decisions.

Which of the traits, skills, and abilities you listed above are your strengths? Which ones could you improve upon?

In what other ways do you think a library leader can have a positive impact in the working lives of others?

## THEORY X, Y, AND Z

In the 1960s, Douglas McGregor broke down the management literature into two theories of human motivation and work behavior: Theory X and Theory Y. While both of these concepts have the word "theory" in their title, they are actually leadership philosophies or approaches to and perceptions of how to manage followers. Theory X is a leadership philosophy that followers must be closely monitored due to their indifference to the work assigned them, and followers are only extrinsically motivated. Theory X views people as mostly passive, lazy, resistant to change, and with little to no ambition. Managing in Theory X comes down to the carrot and the stick. In hard Theory X, management must have a big stick. The only way to get followers to work is through tight control and monitoring of their work and a fear of punishment. Soft Theory X uses a little of the carrot: people will work hard when bribed by a reward for doing the work. Leaders who adhere to Theory X are more autocratic and have a top-down, hierarchical approach to leadership where all major decisions are made by the top formal leader in the organization. Directives on work flow down and reports on work progress flow up. What is interesting about Theory X is that management has a built-in excuse for failure: people. Followers simply did not work hard enough because they are lazy and in some cases outright saboteurs. At the heart of this theory is that people do not like to work and must be forced and coerced against their will to work.

> Lead with compassion. Care about the people you lead and help them get better.

Theory Y is a belief that followers are intrinsically motivated, are the most valuable piece of an organization, and will work up to the standards set for them. Theory Y states that humans have a natural desire to work. In Theory X, followers derive no satisfaction from their work, but in Theory Y followers do derive great satisfaction from their work by achieving organizational and personal goals. In Theory Y, followers will commit to work at the level the work allows them to achieve their goals. Leaders who follow Theory Y have a more democratic, participative, and flat leadership style. Communication flows in many directions, decisions are made at various levels, and the organization uses consensus to move forward on work. Theory Y has no easy excuse for organizational failure. In fact, failure can usually be seen as a fault of the leader, not the followers. McGregor favored Theory Y, and even today Theory Y is taught as the correct way for a leader to think of motivation in followers.

Not too long after Theory X and Theory Y became prominent, some scholars saw the choice between the two as a false dichotomy. What was needed was for leadership to create the right fit between people, jobs, and the organization. The two theories could be seen as being on a spectrum rather than polar opposite choices. Certain situations and people would call for a heavy Theory Y approach—highly skilled, motivated, and experienced people—and other times more Theory X would be needed. The important idea was for a leader to adjust his/her approach based on the people and the job. In one case, a person might be very motivated and in another situation far less motivated. This would become known as situational leadership.

In the 1980s, Theory Z was developed. In Theory Z, leaders provide stability for followers and take great interest in their personal well-being in exchange for follower loyalty. Leaders and organizations should consider looking after and taking care of their employees as their greatest priority. This loyalty is called affective commitment, and research shows that organizations with more affective commitment from their employees are far more successful than those organizations without. This theory is based on studies of Japanese companies where people would spend their entire lives working. At the heart of this theory is organizational culture. A healthy organizational culture is one that fits the work, the organization, and its people. The right culture can greatly increase affective commitment.

Which model—Theory X or Theory Y—do you prefer and why?

_______________

_______________

_______________

_______________

_______________

How might you use each of these approaches in your leadership practice?

_______________

_______________

_______________

_______________

_______________

## CONTINGENCY THEORY AND SITUATIONAL LEADERSHIP

Contingency leadership theory states that not all leaders are right for all environments. In order to be successful, a leader's style must be right for the organizational context, culture, and work performed. Variables that influence and affect leader behavior and success are leader/follower relationships, organizational task structure, and position power. Fred Fiedler was the first to study contingency theory. He developed the ideas of task and relations leaders, and he created the Least Preferred Coworker (LPC) scale as a way to measure leader effectiveness across a range of characteristics. In this theory, leaders are seen as task oriented or relationship oriented. While a few leaders excel at both, this is very difficult, and most leaders will be oriented to one or the other. In one study, 14 percent of results-oriented leaders were considered great, 12 percent of people-oriented leaders were, and 72 percent of leaders who were high at both were considered great leaders. But another study showed that less than 1 percent of leaders scored high in both areas. These activate different areas of the brain that act like a seesaw (Lieberman 2013). The LPC scale can help determine if a leader is a good match for an organization (Hoffman-Miller 2013).

> "The strength of the team is each individual member. The strength of each member is the team."
>
> —PHIL JACKSON

Contingency theory was the first leadership theory to state that leaders are not the sole determinant in their or the organization's success. Followers and the organizational context play an important role as well. At its core is the concept of "fit." If a leader is not the right fit for an organization, then that leader will become stressed and resort to bad coping mechanisms and leadership behaviors. At the heart of contingency leadership is no one right way to lead exists. In fact, no one right way to lead a single organization exists. At one point, an organization may need a more top-down, authoritarian leader to get it through rough financial times or an organizational crisis. During those trying times, this leader will be rated effective by those in the organization, but once the crisis has ended and there is no longer a need for that type of leadership style, that leader will no longer be rated effective. This theory is backed by a large amount of research, but it fails to address a very big, important, and fundamental question: what to do with a leader who is a bad fit for the organization? This theory also speaks to the difficulties a leader has in changing an organizational culture. Presumably, a leader who is selected to change a culture acts and believes differently than the prevailing culture. The catch is that leader will not be deemed a good fit and will be rejected by the existing culture before any changes can be made.

Very similar to contingency theory is situational leadership. In situational leadership, an effective leader is one who is able to change and adapt their approach according to a follower's ability and needs. Leaders have both a directing role in organizations—assigning and guiding work—and a developmental role helping followers grow and succeed. Paul Hersey and Ken Blanchard developed four distinct styles of situational leadership: telling, selling, participating, and delegating. The first two styles are focused on accomplishing goals and completing tasks. A leader can give orders— telling—and expect them to be followed, or they can create buy-in—selling—of a shared goal. The second two styles focus on the growth of followers. Leaders can work alongside and support—participating—the work of followers and the organization. A leader can also delegate the work—delegating—along with decision making to followers. The type of style used is determined by followers' ability and maturity (Campbell 2015). Building on the work of Hersey and Blanchard, Daniel Goleman developed six styles of the situational leader: the coaching leader, who develops followers; the pacesetting leader, who has high expectations of followers; the democratic leader, who values group decision making; the authoritative leader, who is a problem solver; the affiliative leader, who puts the needs of followers above all; and the coercive leader, who gives commands (Campbell 2015).

In order to choose the right style, a leader must evaluate the technical competence and expertise of a person as well as their motivation to perform the work. From there, a leader is able to assign the type of work that would be the best fit (directive) and offer the kind of support needed for a best to develop and succeed (supportive). A long-serving cataloging librarian needs more challenging work than copy cataloging and does not need a detailed explanation of the work they need to do. Doing this kind of work will only frustrate them, and they will never develop. This approach to leadership has been around for a long time, even if it was not called situational leadership, and is a practical approach to leadership. This approach encourages leaders to be flexible in their leadership styles and adapt to different kinds of people in their organization. Situational leadership, however, suffers from a lack of research and is good for one-on-one interactions but not for group interactions.

What pieces, ideas, concepts, etc., do you like from these theories? Dislike? Why?

______________________________________________

______________________________________________

______________________________________________

On your leadership journey, how will you determine how well you fit within an organization's culture, context, and structure? What will you do if you find yourself a bad fit for the position you are in?

How can you adjust your leadership practice to benefit the most people in your library? How can you best determine what a follower needs from you in order to develop and do good work?

## LEADER-MEMBER EXCHANGE

Leader-Member Exchange (LMX) focuses on the relationships a leader builds with individual followers and the subsequent interactions between the leader and the follower. The more positive the interactions, the better the organizational outcomes. Better interactions also mean less turnover, better annual evaluation ratings, and more affective commitment. In short, the better leader/follower relations, the better the organization performs and the more easily the organization meets its outcomes and goals. These interactions and relationships are sometimes referred to as "dyadic relationships." In small organizations, a leader could conceivably have a relationship with everyone in the organization. Assuming these relationships are all positive, this is beneficial to everyone. But in larger organizations, a leader cannot build and maintain relationships with everyone in an organization, let alone have a positive relationship with everyone. Leaders must choose with whom to have relationships. This choice is based on many things, not the least of which are a follower's work ethic, skills and abilities, values, and potential.

In LMX, followers can be divided into the "in group" and the "out group." The followers who a part of the in group enjoy better and stronger relationships with the organizational leader than those followers who are members of the out group. Followers are divided into these groups in stages. The first stage is called role taking. The leader assesses a new follower and formulates ideas and assumptions about him/her. Next, the role-making stage, the new follower is assigned work, and their work progress and quality either supports or does not support the initial leader assumption. Finally, the follower is assigned to the in group or the out group in the routinization stage (Miller 2013). Those who are members of the in group receive more attention, support, responsibility, and freedom. These are the people who act as informal leaders within the organization and will ultimately go on to be formal leaders in other organizations. In exchange for the freedom and mentoring, the members of the in group are expected to work harder and do more than members of the out group. The members of the out group are treated in a more transactional way by the organization's leadership. Both the leader and the follower adhere to the minimum expected of them in performing their duties. This is the "exchange" of leader-member exchange. Individuals who exceed their expectations and requirements will receive more from leadership in exchange for their work than those who simply meet their requirements. The in group, then, are those in the organization who go above and beyond what is required of them, and those in the out group complete their assigned work tasks, nothing more and nothing less. Members of the in group see the organizational leader as a true leader, while the out group thinks of the organizational leader as more of an authority figure.

LMX relies heavily on followers. The formation of groups and the level of exchange are based on their efforts and potential. The drawback to LMX is the development of in groups and out groups and how followers are assigned to those groups. Group membership can be heavily influenced by a leader's bias and can lead to problems with discrimination and lack of diversity. This bias can come at any stage of the group assignation process. A leader could develop unrealistic expectations, be subject to confirmation bias in judging their work, and fail to reassess a follower's current work and instead rely on past behavior. In addition, the in group can become a clique within the organization with too much power, whether real or perceived. The reality, though, is that a leader only has so much time, resources, and energy, and he/she must spend them in the way that will give them the best return on investment. Spending more resources on those followers who have demonstrated a high work ethic, commitment to the organization, and the ability to become leaders themselves is far more efficient than trying to coach a mediocre employee to greatness.

In order to influence someone, you need to have a relationship with them. Build relationships with everyone you can, especially with people you might not like. Those are the people you often need to influence the most.

What pieces, ideas, concepts, etc., do you like from this theory? Dislike? Why?

What pieces, ideas, concepts, etc., work well with your definition and theory? Why?

## TRANSFORMATIONAL LEADERSHIP

Transformational leaders use the "Four I's"—idealized influence, individualized consideration, inspirational motivation, and intellectual stimulation—to improve organizational effectiveness, facilitate long-lasting change, create personal relationships, and develop leaders throughout the organization. Transformational leadership exists on a leadership spectrum consisting of laissez-faire, transactional, and transformational leadership. Laissez-faire is the absence of leadership. While some situations exist—not getting involved in personal differences in a large organization—in which the use of laissez-faire leadership is preferable, the absence of leadership is generally not a good leadership practice.

Transactional leadership is not bad, per se. Even the greatest transformational leaders need the most basic transactional skills like setting goals and rewarding performance to be successful. Transactional leaders can and do move organizations in the right direction, but only so far. Transactional leaders do not inspire new ways of thinking and doing, nor do they develop leaders within the organization. Most transactional leaders do not know how to be transformational. Transactional and transformational leaders have different mindsets (Avolio 2011). Transactional leaders appeal to the self-interest of followers, while transformational leaders motivate followers to think of the greater organizational good. Transactional leaders provide positive reinforcement of good organizational behavior and negative reinforcement of bad organizational behavior. They are trusted when they show a record of keeping their word, but transformational leaders are given a deeper trust. Transactional leaders create environments where risk taking is discouraged and followers do not innovate (Avolio 2011).

Through the use of the the Four I's —idealized influence, act as role model; inspirational motivation, provide meaning to the work of the organization; intellectual stimulation, encourage creativity; individualized consideration, provide mentoring—transformational leaders are able to increase organizational effectiveness, follower satisfaction, and organizational effort (Bass and Avolio 1994). Transformational leadership positively influences creativity and intrinsic motivation and psychologically empowers employees. Overall, transformational leadership enhances organizational innovation (Gumusluoglu and Ilsev 2009). Transformational leaders have been found to be better communicators and have higher agreement on organizational goals (Berson and Avolio 2004). Transformational leaders constantly emphasize organizational mission and vision, encourage followers to view problems and situations from multiple different and new perspectives, and ask that followers think more about the actions that will benefit the organization than those that will only affect them (Bass and Avolio 1994). Through the use of the Four I's, transformational leaders build personal, deep relationships with those in the organization. These relationships have a long-lasting positive influence (Martin 2017).

The role of followers is critical in transformational leadership. Transactional leaders work with followers in a series of exchanges; followers meet goals and are given rewards by the transactional leader (Burns 1978). Leaders and followers decide what are appropriate goals and rewards. Without the cooperation of followers, a transactional leader could not succeed. Transformational leaders are just as dependent on followers, if not more so, than transactional leaders. "Transcendent followership" requires followers to display certain competencies in relationships with others, build on their strengths, and be accepting of change. Without transcendent followers, transformational leadership is less likely to succeed (Cunha, Rego, Clegg, and Neves 2013). Follower development affects leadership style. Followers who are intrinsically motivated, principled, and empowered are better suited to transformational leaders. The leader/follower relationship in the transformational model is based on the strengths, not the weaknesses, of the follower (Dvir and Shamir 2003).

Transformational leadership has many benefits for followers. They develop and grow as professionals and leaders, change is easier with a transformational leader, and followers of transformational leaders are more satisfied with leadership, the organization, and their overall work life. Followers with high "growth need" and desire for autonomy rate transformational leaders as being more effective and rate their own satisfaction as higher than followers with low "growth need" and desire for autonomy (Goodwin 2001). But it can also be negative for followers as well. Transformational leaders can have poor organizational outcomes, and, without the proper ethics, transformational leaders can take advantage of the power and use it for their own selfish gain.

Transformational leadership is very pie in the sky in what it asks of leaders. No one will ever be great at all four of the I's and definitely not all the time. Interestingly, some research suggests that improving emotional intelligence makes a leader more transformational. In addition, the overly broad nature of the theory makes it difficult to define. Transactional leadership is a perfectly fine leadership style when the external environment is stable. Perhaps transformational leaders—who are few and far between—are only needed at certain times. Maybe even transformational leaders can be counterproductive in times of stability. Further, without solid checks and balances and firm grounding in ethical behavior, transformational leadership can become exclusive and authoritarian, leading to manipulation, coercion, and abuse of power. Lacking critical pushback, transformational leaders can undertake change at too rapid a rate leading to burnout in personnel. A leader's vision can also be misguided, taking the organization in a direction that could prove to be harmful in the long term. Transformational leadership strongly emphasizes a leader's personality, which is formed at an early age. This not only makes the necessary transformational traits more difficult to learn, but the emphasis on personality, appeal to emotion, and influence on followers can create a cult of personality. This can attract the wrong type of people to leadership for the wrong reasons.

With all that being said, the Four I's have a lot of benefits for leaders, followers, and organizations, starting with idealized influence. Being a role model for organizational values is a canon trait of leadership theories. As a leader, you set the tone for how others in the organization act, behave, and work. Through idealized influence, you can influence followers' mindsets and behavior and create a strongly shared mission and vision. As a leader, you need to act like you are constantly being watched because you are. Individualized consideration means leaders must get to know people in their organization, understand what they want from their job and their career, and treat them accordingly. Trying to mentor someone to be a leader when they are not interested in being a leader is a waste of time. Regardless of their needs, you can help folks set and reach goals and provide the support that is needed for them. Through individualized consideration, leaders build relationships that are crucial for organizational success. Inspirational motivation is a little more challenging. Motivating another person can be difficult, and motivation is fleeting. A better way to look at this may be to provide proper recognition, feedback, and rewards for work well done. Whether it is a thank you or an awards luncheon, people want to have their work recognized and appreciated. Intellectual stimulation is also difficult for leaders. Here, you should focus on creating an environment where followers feel free to take risks, try something new, and most importantly fail. This can be a long and daunting task that is made easier through relationships and mutual trust.

Do you see yourself as more of a transactional or transformational leader? How can you make adjustments in your mindset and style to become more transformational?

What pieces, ideas, concepts, etc., do you like from this theory? Dislike? Why?

What pieces, ideas, concepts, etc., work well with your definition and theory? Why?

______________________________________________________________________

______________________________________________________________________

______________________________________________________________________

______________________________________________________________________

______________________________________________________________________

______________________________________________________________________

## EMOTIONAL INTELLIGENCE

Emotional intelligence has been a hot topic in leadership since it was first written about almost 30 years ago. Emotional intelligence consists of four concepts: self-awareness, self-management, social awareness, and relationship management. Emotionally intelligent individuals are more likely to emerge as leaders of groups and organizations. Further, emotionally intelligent leaders are better at their overall job, and those in the organization rate their leadership skills as higher than their non-emotionally intelligent colleagues (Sheldon, Ames, and Dunning 2014). Emotional intelligence was found to be "twice as important" as IQ and "technical skills" (Goleman 2004). Leaders who have high emotional intelligence are better at overcoming obstacles and persevering through difficult times to achieve goals, are perceived as being better leaders, and manage personal relationships better. Emotionally intelligent leaders are more innovative in the services they develop and are better negotiators (Humphrey 2013).

The emotions that fill organizations can be enormous and overwhelming. Some research has found organizational change produces emotions akin with the emotions of death. These powerful emotions are what fuel resistance to change (Vakola, Tsaousis, and Nikolaou 2004). Emotional culture—the emotions displayed and prevalent throughout the organization like love, fear, anger, and happiness—are just as important to a library as the cognitive culture. The emotional culture dictates how people respond to each other and to leadership. Leaders can play a big part in creating this culture. The emotions they exhibit—even in unintentional ways—help set the library's emotional tone (Martin 2018a).

Peter Salovey and John Mayer were two of the first researchers to study and write about emotional intelligence. They defined emotional intelligence as "the subset of social intelligence that involves the ability to monitor one's own and others' feelings and emotions, to discriminate among them and to use this information to guide one's thinking and actions" (Salovey and Mayer 1990, 190). Emotionally intelligent individuals are better at expressing their own feelings, understanding the emotional states of others, and communicating both verbally and nonverbally. Emotionally intelligent people are better at "flexible planning" (making future plans with multiple outcomes), "creative thinking," "mood redirected attention" (drawn to problems of a greater importance in a crisis), and "motivating emotions" (Salovey and Mayer 1990, 199–200).

## Self-Awareness

The first piece of emotional intelligence is self-awareness. Leaders who have high self-awareness understand what events and people have shaped them, have a strong values system, have a better grasp of how to better themselves, and have large goals and long-term objectives. Self-aware leaders are better at clarifying their values and aligning those values with their actions. When you act out of alignment with your espoused values, you are a hypocrite, which can lead to a lack of trust from your library. Self-aware leaders also understand their energy and work rhythms. This might seem like a small thing, but being aware of when you work best and what types of activities energize or drain you help you perform at your best. If you know a meeting is going to drain you, then schedule light work after it. If you are more alert after lunch, then plan on making important decisions then.

Leaders with higher self-awareness also better understand their strengths and limitations. No leader can do everything. You need to surround yourself with people who complement your abilities and fill in your gaps. Are you good with people but bad with systems? Great with numbers, data, and budgets but disorganized and bad about deadlines? This self-knowledge will help you fill out your leadership team. Self-aware leaders are better at facilitating change. Their awareness allows them to keep their emotions in check and reflect on their work and actions. Self-aware leaders also frequently ask for assessment of their work, and they try to view themselves as others see them. Because self-aware leaders are in control of themselves, they are more motivating and can more easily broach demanding topics and problems within the organization and the change process (Higgs and Rowland 2010). The key to self-awareness is introspection that honestly explains behaviors, motivations, strengths, weaknesses, and overall performance and capacity as a leader.

## Self-Management

Self-awareness informs self-management. Knowing when is the best time for you to make a decision and why you are making a decision are key to leadership, and self-awareness and self-management allow you to do both. Self-management can help in ways we may not think about much. Self-management means you do not have to give an immediate answer. You can wait until you have the time to think about it and feel comfortable with your decision. Much of our communication is nonverbal, and self-management allows us to control our nonverbal communication. As a leader, you cannot sit in a meeting and sigh, roll your eyes, or cross your arms and slouch. It also allows you to moderate your responses and be consistent in those responses. If you respond sweetly and gently one moment and fly into a rage the next, then no one will think you are approachable. Unstable leaders are not trusted because their moods are too erratic. Instability can also lead to burnout, especially as it relates to work-life balance (Goleman 2006).

> Do not commit to a course of action without knowing the whole situation. You can show concern for a person and their situation without agreeing to a solution until you know more.

Self-management is key in creating a healthy work-life balance. In today's constantly connected world, the boundaries between work and social life are blurred and sometimes are nonexistent. On top of this, the expectation, especially for leaders, is faster responses at all times of the day or night. This can lead to high levels of stress and burnout and ruined personal relationships. An emotionally intelligent leader recognizes the need for balance but also understands this will not be perfect. Sometimes work takes over and sometimes personal life does. An emotionally intelligent leader knows when to shift priorities and monitors self. An emotionally intelligent leader also monitors others to make sure they are not burning themselves out with work in order to get ahead or be promoted.

## Social Awareness

These first two pieces are about us and how we act as leaders. The next two pieces become more about others in the organization, therefore they become a little trickier. Empathy is a key component of not just emotional intelligence but also being human. Empathy allows us to understand and connect with other human beings. High-empathy leaders are better motivators, create a less stressful workplace, have more satisfied customers, and lead creative and innovative organizations (Humphrey 2013). The more empathy displayed by a leader, the better relationships exist between leader and follower. These better relationships lead to a more effective organization, happier followers, and better leadership (Mashud, Yukl, and Prussia 2010). In a study of leaders across 38 countries, researchers found the more empathic a leader was the higher the follower rated his/her leadership. In other words, followers found the most empathetic leaders to be the most effective leaders (Sadri, Weber, and Gentry 2011).

Some people are naturally more empathetic than others, and some people grew up in environments where empathy was readily shown to them, making it easier for them to cultivate and express empathy. But empathy can be learned and developed and is an important tool for a leader. Empathetic listening allows you to not only listen—really listen to what another is actually saying—but also make them feel as if they are being heard. Again, a large part of communication is nonverbal, and empathy helps you hear what is not being said. Greater levels of self-awareness make us more open to our environment and others. This leads to greater empathy and understanding.

Organizational awareness—understanding the organization's groups, cliques, culture, and politics—is very important for a leader. When it comes to an organization's emotional culture, a leader can be either resonant or dissonant. Resonant leaders use empathy with their followers and are emotionally attuned to others in their organization. Resonant leaders promote collaboration and innovation. Dissonant leaders fail to use empathy with followers and colleagues and give off negative emotions. Dissonant leaders create "anger, fear, or even sullen silence" (Goleman, Boyatzs, and McKee 2013).

## Relationship Management

Building relationships is key for a leader, and empathy is what good leaders use to build relationships of mutual trust. Relationships both inside and outside the library are critical to your success. In a study of several hundred employees across various organizational settings, researchers found leader/follower relationships do more to build trust than a leader's personal characteristics or a leader's ability to define the organization's mission, vision, and goals (Hernandez, Long, and Sitkin 2014). Better relationships between leaders and followers lead to better "organizational citizenship behaviors." Organizational citizenship behavior can be described as being very involved in an organization and job beyond one's job description to make positive contributions to the organization, which is important in today's ever-changing organizations (Bowler, Halbesleben, and Paul 2010). Organizational members who identify strongly with a group have a better relationship with the group's leader than those members who do not identify with a group (Steffens, Haslam, and Reicher 2014).

Leaders and followers have an "interdependent" relationship. Followers choose who to follow, and leaders need followers and must have a good relationship with them in order to succeed (Kean and Haycock-Stuart 2011). A healthy, positive relationship between leader and follower, one that takes into account each individual's past, has a significant influence on the development of "authentic relationships" between leader and follower (Hinojosa, McCauley, Randolph-Seng, and Gardner 2014). This brings us to the role of followers in emotional intelligence. Does it take emotional intelligence to respond to emotional intelligence? Do you need high empathy to respond to empathy? How do you mentor someone with no or little self-awareness? Empathy may be the biggest piece that is needed in both followers and leaders. It does take empathy to perceive and respond to empathy. A lack of empathy in followers can result in responding to leader empathy with mistrust and conspiratorial worry. The research on emotional intelligence in followers is slim. The value of emotionally intelligent organizations has been written about, but there is no research on how rare or common they are.

How would you rate your emotional intelligence in the four areas? How could you improve in each area?

What pieces, ideas, concepts, etc., do you like from this theory? Dislike? Why?

What pieces, ideas, concepts, etc., work well with your definition and theory? Why?

______________________________________________

______________________________________________

______________________________________________

______________________________________________

______________________________________________

______________________________________________

## AUTHENTIC LEADERSHIP

Authentic leadership is a concept with many definitions. To a lot of people, authentic leadership is an "I know it when I see it" idea. Most definitions of what an authentic leader is include finding and speaking with your own voice, being true to your own thoughts, feelings, and emotions, and leading with your values. Dependence and reliance on typologies, skills, and competencies of leadership may hinder the development of authentic leadership (Lawler 2005). Bill George, who has done much to popularize authentic leadership, defines authentic leaders as purpose-driven, values-centered, compassionate, relationship builders, and self-disciplined with a strong service ethic. Most importantly, they are themselves in every way in every situation, made easier by their strong sense of purpose (George 2003, ). Daniel Goleman defines being authentic as being "the same person to others as you are to yourself" (Goleman 2013, 53). This last part, always being yourself, is far trickier for a leader than it initially seems. Leaders must "be leader," but more importantly they must "do leader." In order to be truly effective, a leader must "do leadership," that is, they must act like a leader and do the things a leader does. This can include attending late-night and weekend events, developing donors, making difficult personnel decisions, and performing a host of other duties that might not be appealing to everyone but must be done. The other part of doing leadership is to act according to the cultural assumptions of leadership. Leaders are expected to act, talk, and walk a certain way according to their unique organizational cultures. What one culture thinks makes a great leader may be viewed as bad leadership by another. This is made more difficult by the fact that it is not whether a leader has a trait or skill, but if followers perceive they have that trait or skill and whether it manifests itself in a positive or negative way (Popper 2012). Our leadership identity then is composed of how we see, think of, and perceive ourselves, and how followers see, think of, and perceive us. Further, being yourself is more difficult for groups of people who tend to not occupy many leadership positions like women, African Americans, and Latino/as to name a few.

A better way to approach authentic leadership is through values. An authentic leader has a strong values system and strong understanding of his/her values. Authentic leaders then act in accordance with those values in everything they do. In order to be effective, this requires a leader to be both self-aware and self-managing, two of the four key components of emotional intelligence. Self-awareness can be difficult for people in leadership positions. Leaders must conform in certain ways to cultural expectations, which may require compromise. Self-awareness requires reflection, which takes time to think about actions and outcomes. Leaders, however, are routinely short of time in which to reflect. Maybe the biggest obstacle to self-awareness is the higher a leader climbs in the organizational hierarchy and the more powerful he/she becomes, the fewer and fewer people who are willing to be honest with him/her. This lack of honest feedback means leaders might not only be unaware they are acting hypocritically, boorishly, and tyrannically, but they might also be unaware they are being bad leaders.

> "Whatever you are, be a good one."
>
> —ABRAHAM LINCOLN

In order to be authentic, a leader must engage in "actively being," which is achieved through self-awareness and intense reflection (Lawler 2004). This self-examination is not limited to values. Much of leadership is about meaning. Leaders create organizational meaning in order to influence followers, and leaders also create their own leadership meaning. Why a leader is leading and what they want to do as a leader is critical for any leader to know about themselves. Each leader must define organizational meaning and his/her own leadership meaning by choosing from almost limitless options and then being personally responsible for those choices. The only unallowable option is to not choose an option (Lawler 2004). An authentic leader is also one who has chosen his/her own meaning through thoughtful reflection and is responsible for and wholly committed to those decisions. An authentic leader is a true believer in their message and meaning, both of which are based on the leader's values.

What pieces, ideas, concepts, etc., do you like from this theory? Dislike? Why?

What pieces, ideas, concepts, etc., work well with your definition and theory? Why?

## SERVANT LEADERSHIP

Servant leaders do not lead for the money, glory, power, or fame that may come from leading. They do not put themselves first. Instead, servant leaders put followers first. Servant leaders are servants of their followers. They strive to serve them and help them grow and achieve both personally and professionally. Servant leadership was popularized by Robert Greenleaf, who described it as the idea that leaders should serve those in the organization, put the needs of others first, share power throughout the organization, and help those in the

> "You have to be willing to serve someone else."
>
> —NICK SABAN

organization become the best they can be. Greenleaf wrote, "The servant-leader is servant first. It begins with the natural feeling that one wants to serve. Then conscious choice brings one to aspire to lead" (Greenleaf 2002, 27). Greenleaf went on to describe the main traits of a servant leader. To Greenleaf, a servant leader has a vision and creates trust; listens first; empathizes, but does not accept poor performance; "has a sense for the unknowable and be able to foresee the unforeseeable"; uses foresight; is open and aware; is persuasive; and builds community (Greenleaf 2002, 35). The real test of servant leader is as Greenleaf described it:

> Do those served grow as persons? Do they, while being served, become healthier, wiser, freer, more autonomous, more likely themselves to become servants? And, what is the effect on the least privileged in society? Will they benefit or at least not be further deprived? (Greenleaf 2002, 27)

Greenleaf based much of servant leadership on teachings from the Christian church. The use of "servant leadership" is very popular in religious organizations, but the term is seldom used in the corporate world. But just because the term is not used much does not mean leaders of all types and walks are not engaging in it daily. Many leaders are adamant about putting people first in their organizations. The difficulty in using servant leadership can be too much focus on people and too little on mission and organizational outcomes. The phrase used earlier in the book "people first, mission always" puts this in perspective. Leaders have to be able to balance taking care of the needs of those in the organization with effectively running the organization.

Servant leadership does not have much empirical research to support it. It is not an easy concept to define and, therefore, measure. Leaders are expected to have a knack for knowing what is unknowable. This is hard enough to do as a leader and even harder, if not impossible, to measure as a researcher. Followers play an important role in servant leadership. The servant leader helps followers transcend their present performance and environment to become the best they can be. This assumes that followers are not already performing at their best—in this case the servant leader would be focused on how to maintain that level of work—and, if they are not performing at their best, that they want to move beyond the status quo. Another drawback to servant leadership is always putting others first. Leaders take a lot of flak from just about every direction. They tend to have short tenures and sacrifice a lot of their personal life to lead. Leaders should sometimes put themselves first and enjoy the occasional perk of being a leader. This does not mean taking three-hour lunches every day and four-day weekends every week, but rather having the close parking spot and the nicer office.

What pieces, ideas, concepts, etc., do you like from this theory? Dislike? Why?

What pieces, ideas, concepts, etc., work well with your definition and theory? Why?

five

# Developing a Leadership Practice

## REEXAMINATION OF LEADERSHIP DEFINITION AND THEORY

In this final chapter, let's return to your personal leadership analysis, definition of leadership, and theory of leadership, and think about how your ideas have or have not changed over the course of reading this book. Review your definition of leadership. How would you alter your definition? Which ideas, concepts, or definitions covered in this book would you add to your definition? Which concepts or ideas would you remove from your definition? Which traits, skills, and abilities would you add to or remove from your personal leadership analysis? How has your theory of how a leader should act and leadership manifest itself in a library changed? Finally, what aspects of the theories covered in this book do you want to incorporate into your theory?

**Leadership Community**

Find and build a community of people who will support and nurture your leadership practice through mentoring, coaching, and feedback.

Write your revised definition of leadership below. If your definition has not changed, then that is fine as long as you have taken the time to deeply engage with the material presented in this book.

Revised Important Leadership Traits, Skills, and Abilities. Copy your original list. Are there any traits, skills, and abilities you would now add to the list? Any you would remove?

1.
2.
3.
4.
5.
6.
7.
8.
9.
10.

Write your revised theory of leadership below. If your theory has not changed, then that is fine as long as you have taken the time to deeply engage with the material presented in this book.

Using your own revised definition, theory, and list of traits and skills, assess your:

1. Strengths as a Leader (Internal-Helpful)

________________________________________

________________________________________

________________________________________

________________________________________

________________________________________

2. Weaknesses as a Leader (Internal-Hurtful)

________________________________________

________________________________________

________________________________________

________________________________________

________________________________________

________________________________________

3. Opportunities to Practice, Learn, and Improve as a Leader (External-Helpful)

________________________________________

________________________________________

________________________________________

________________________________________

________________________________________

4. Threats to Your Ability to Develop as a Leader (External-Hurtful)

Write your revised leadership USP below. Taking in all that you have read and done, would you change your leadership slogan from chapter one? If so, what would your new one be?

## LEADERSHIP GOALS

Using your leadership purpose, mission, and vision as guides, set big, scary leadership goals. These should be the types of goals that make you excited and nervous. Just writing them down should scare you and motivate you. Do not worry about time lines or SMART goals. These should be the big, overarching goals that give your leadership journey a direction. Striving for these goals should make you better, so not reaching them will not make you a failure. These goals should align with your leadership purpose, mission, and vision, and, most importantly, they need to align with your personal and professional values. Take time to review your leadership purpose, vision, mission, and values before writing your goals. Would you change any of them now? Thinking about your goals, where do you want to go as a library leader? What do you want to learn and experience? Spend some time thinking about these and come back to them as needed. As time goes by, update and revise your goals as needed. Remember, if you want to be successful, then all your goals must be based on your purpose as a leader.

Write your leadership goals below.

______________________________

______________________________

______________________________

______________________________

______________________________

## DEVELOP A LEADERSHIP PLAN AND PRACTICE

You now have your definition and theory of leadership and your leadership goals. Take it a step further and develop a plan of practice. This plan of practice is your way to become a leader if you are not one already or to become a better leader. Your plan will allow you to take the ideas you have developed in this book and put them into action.

How can you apply your definition and theory to your leadership work?

______________________________

______________________________

______________________________

______________________________

______________________________

In what areas do you want to improve?

What steps can you take to improve your skills?

How will you demonstrate your leadership value?

And maybe most importantly, what leadership roles will you take on? If you are already in a leadership position, then how will you use what you have learned in this book to inform your leadership practice?

What can you do to become a better leader?

Make time for reflection on your leadership journey. Take the time to critically review your work to make sure you are staying true to your purpose. Come back to this work and the answers you gave. Is what you wrote still working for you? Are your definition, goals, and practice plan still applicable to you in your current situation? Go back and reread the book and revise your answers so as to best help you where you are in your leadership journey.

# go lead!

You have just completed a lot of work and thinking about your leadership journey. Piecing it all together, the work that lies in front of you may seem daunting. Do not panic. You do not need to complete it all at once. In fact, neither you nor the greatest leader who ever lived can do it all at once. Instead, focus on breaking your leadership work into small pieces. What skills do you want to improve this fiscal quarter? How can you make better use of your values this semester? In this way, you will improve with each step you take. With the work you do each day, you will become a better leader, and the better leader you become, the bigger the work you can do and the bolder the change you can make.

As a leader, you can do great work, but you must remember that leaders do not act alone. To be effective as a leader, you need to be aware of what you can control and who you can influence. When you encounter obstacles, you have to know when to fight and when to find another way around them. Leadership takes place in the interactions between leader and follower that occur within a culture specific to your library. For these interactions to be successful, you must know your followers and know your culture. Remember to be flexible in your approach to leadership. Set high standards for yourself, but do not set impossible ones. Use your self-awareness and empathy to judge how leadership interactions go and improve as needed. Work to understand people, their wants and needs, and help them accordingly. As people and situations change, adjust accordingly.

The problem with most of the leadership literature is that it indulges in the romance of leadership, which can cause us to question our effectiveness as leaders and doubt our abilities. If you have confidence and strength and act according to your purpose, then you are being an effective leader. Embrace the responsibility of leadership, its privileges, and its burdens. Always accept blame and give recognition. Find new influences and meaningful challenges in order to not become stale. Finally, the world will not be changed in one fell swoop. The journey to meaningful change and impact is long and made up of small victories. Never forget to celebrate and enjoy what you have accomplished and how far you have come.

> "[Leadership] is a way of life for those who know who they are and are willing to be their best to create the life they want to live."
>
> —KATHLEEN SCHAFER

# bibliography


Avolio, Bruce. 2011. *Full Range Leadership Development*. Los Angeles: Sage.

Bass, Bernard, and Bruce Avolio. 1994. Introduction. In *Improving Organizational Effectiveness through Transactional Leadership*, edited by Bernard Bass and Bruce Avolio, 1–9. Thousand Oaks, CA: Sage.

Berson, Yair, and Bruce Avolio. 2004. "Transformational Leadership and the Dissemination of Organizational Goals: A Case Study of a Telecommunication Firm." *The Leadership Quarterly* 15 (5): 625–46.

Bowler, Matthew, Jonathon Halbesleben, and Jeff Paul. 2010. "If You're Close with the Leader, You Might Be a Brown Nose: The Role of Leader-Member Relationships in Follower, Leader, and Coworker Attributions of Organizational Citizenship Behavior Motives." *Human Resource Management Review* 20 (4): 309–16.

Burns, James MacGregor. 1978. *Leadership*. New York: Harper and Row.

Cameron, Kim and Robert Quinn. 2011. *Diagnosing and changing organizational culture*. San Francisco: Jossey-Bass.

Campbell, Josephine. 2015. "Situational Leadership Theory." *Salem Press Encyclopedia*.

Cunha, Miguel Pina e, Aremenio Rego, Stewart Clegg, and Pedro Neves. 2013. "The Case for Transcendent Followership." *Leadership* 9 (1): 87–106.

Dvir, Taly, and Boas Shamir. 2003. "Follower Developmental Characteristics as Predicting Transformational Leadership: A Longitudinal Field Study." *The Leadership Quarterly* 14 (3): 327–44.

George, Bill. 2003. *Authentic Leadership: Rediscovering the Secrets to Creating Lasting Value*. San Francisco: Jossey-Bass.

Goleman, Daniel. 2004. "What Makes a Leader?" *Harvard Business Review* 82 (1): 82–91.

_____. 2006. *Emotional Intelligence*. New York: Bantam Books.

_____. 2013. "The Focused Leader." *Harvard Business Review* 91 (12): 50–60.

Goleman, Daniel, Richard Boyatzs, and Annie McKee. 2013. *Primal Leadership: Unleashing the Power of Emotional Intelligence*. Boston: Harvard Business Review Press.

Goodwin, Vicki. 2001. "Follower Motive Patterns as Situational Moderators for Transformational Leadership Effectiveness." *Journal of Managerial Issues* 13 (2): 196–211.

Greenleaf, Robert. 2002. *Servant Leadership*. New York: Paulist Press.

Gumusluoglu, Lale, and Arzu Ilsev. 2009. "Transformational Leadership, Creativity, and Organizational Innovation." *Journal of Business Research* 62 (4): 461–73.

Hernandez, Morela, Chris Long, and Sim Sitkin. 2014. "Cultivating Follower Trust: Are All Leader Behaviors Equally Influential?" *Organization Studies* 35 (12): 1,867–92.

Higgs, Malcolm, and Deborah Rowland. 2010. "Emperors with Clothes On: The Role of Self-Awareness in Developing Effective Change Leadership." *Journal of Change Management* 10 (4): 369–85.

Hinojosa, Amanda, Kelly McCauley, Brandon Randolph-Seng, and William Gardner. 2014. "Leader and Follower Attachment Styles: Implications for Authentic Leader-Follower Relationships." *The Leadership Quarterly* 25 (3): 595–610.

Hoffman-Miller, Patricia. 2013. "Contingency Theory." *Salem Press Encyclopedia*.

Humphrey, Ronald. 2013. "The Benefits of Emotional Intelligence and Empathy to Entrepreneurship." *Entrepreneurship Research Journal* 3 (3): 287–94.

Kean, Susanne, and Elaine Haycock-Stuart. 2011. "Understanding the Relationship Between Followers and Leaders." *Nursing Management* 18 (8): 31–5.

Lawler, John. 2005. "The Essence of Leadership? Existentialism and Leadership." *Leadership* 1 (2): 215–31.

———. 2004. "Meaning and Being: Existentialist Concepts in Leadership." *International Journal of Management Concepts and Philosophy* 1 (1): 61–72.

Lieberman, Matthew. 2013. "Should Leaders Focus on Results, or on People?" Harvard Business Review Online. https://hbr.org/2013/12/should-leaders-focus-on-results-or-on-people.

Martin, Jason. 2017. "Personal Relationships and Professional Results: The Positive Impact of Transformational Leaders on Academic Librarians." *Journal of Academic Librarianship*, 43 (2): 108–15.

———. 2018a. "Emotional Intelligence, Emotional Culture, and Library Leadership." *Library Leadership & Management* 33 (1): 1–14.

———. 2018b. "What Do Academic Librarians Value in a Leader? Reflections on Past Positive Library Leaders and a Consideration of Future Library Leaders." *College & Research Libraries* 79 (6): 799–821.

———. 2019. "The Leadership/Followership Process: A New Understanding of Library Leadership." *Journal of Academic Librarianship* 45 (1): 15–21.

Mashud, Rubina, Gary Yukl, and Greg Prussia. 2010. "Leader Empathy, Ethical Leadership, and Relations-Oriented Behaviors as Antecedents of Leader -Member Exchange Quality." *Journal of Managerial Psychology* 25 (6): 561–77.

Miller, Shari Parsons. 2013. "Leader Member Exchange." *Salem Press Encyclopedia*.

Popper, Micha. 2012. *Fact and Fantasy about Leadership*. Northampton, MA: Edward Elgar.

Sadri, Golnaz, Todd Weber, and William Gentry. 2011. "Empathic Emotion and Leadership Performance: An Empirical Analysis Across 38 Countries." *The Leadership Quarterly* 22 (5): 818–30.

Salovey, Peter, and John Mayer. 1990. "Emotional Intelligence." *Imagination, Cognition, and Personality* 9 (3): 185–211.

Schein, Edgar. 2004. *Organizational Culture and Leadership*. San Francisco: Jossey-Bass.

Sheldon, Oliver, D. Covalt Ames, and Daniel Dunning. 2014. "Emotionally Unskilled, Unaware, and Uninterested in Learning More: Reactions to Feedback about Deficits in Emotional Intelligence." *Journal of Applied Psychology* 99 (1): 125–37.

Steffens, Niklas, Alexander Haslam, and Stephen Reicher. 2014. "Up Close and Personal: Evidence That Shared Social Identity Is a Basis for the 'Special' Relationship That Binds Followers to Leaders." *The Leadership Quarterly* 25 (2): 296–313.

Taylor, Bill. 2017. *5 Questions to Ask about Corporate Culture to Get Beyond the Usual Meaningless Blather*. https://hbr.org/2017/06/5-questions-to-ask-about-corporate-culture-to-get-beyond-the-usual-meaningless-blather.

Vakola, Maria, Ioannis Tsaousis, and Ioannis Nikolaou. 2004. "The Role of Emotional Intelligence and Personality Variables on Attitude toward Organizational Change." *Journal of Managerial Psychology* 19 (2): 88–110.

# notes